Dyslexia

Alexis Roumanis

e Explore other books at:
WWW.ENGAGEBOOKS.COM

VANCOUVER, B.C.

e WWW.ENGAGEBOOKS.COM

Dyslexia: Understand Your Mind and Body
Roumanis, Alexis 1982 -
Text © 2023 Engage Books
Design © 2023 Engage Books

Edited by: Ashley Lee and Melody Sun
Design by: Mandy Christiansen

Text set in Montserrat Regular.
Chapter headings set in Hobgoblin.

FIRST EDITION / FIRST PRINTING

This book is not meant to replace the advice of a medical professional or be a tool for diagnosis. It is an educational tool to help children understand what they or other people are going through.

LIBRARY AND ARCHIVES CANADA CATALOGUING IN PUBLICATION

Title: Dyslexia / Alexis Roumanis and Dayna Roumanis.
Names: Roumanis, Alexis, author. | Roumanis, Dayna, author.
Description: Series statement: Understand your mind and body

Identifiers: Canadiana (print) 20230506836 | Canadiana (ebook) 20230506844
ISBN 978-1-77878-165-0 (hardcover)
ISBN 978-1-77878-166-7 (softcover)
ISBN 978-1-77878-167-4 (epub)
ISBN 978-1-77878-168-1 (pdf)
ISBN 978-1-77878-111-7 (audio)

Subjects:
LCSH: Dyslexia—Juvenile literature.
LCSH: Dyslexic children—Juvenile literature.
LCSH: Dyslexia—Treatment—Juvenile literature.

Classification: LCC RJ496.A5 R68 2023 | DDC J618.92/8553—DC23

This project has been made possible in part by the Government of Canada.

Canada

Contents

What Is Dyslexia?

Dyslexia is a learning difference that affects how people read, write, speak, and spell. It is not a disease, and it does not mean someone is not smart. Dyslexia can make it hard to read quickly and **accurately**.

KEY WORD

Accurately: doing something correctly without mistakes.

There are different types of dyslexia. Some people may have trouble matching sounds with letters. Others might have a hard time remembering words. Dyslexia can also make it difficult to put words in the right order when writing or speaking.

Phonological dyslexia is when people struggle to decode or sound out words.

ee
green
feet
see

ea
eat
clean
seat

What Causes Dyslexia?

Scientists often do not know what causes dyslexia, but they believe it can run in families. It is not something that can be caught from someone else. A person's brain **processes** information differently if they have dyslexia.

KEY WORD

Processes: the steps or actions taken to make or understand something.

Dyslexia can develop from a brain injury or disease. This is the only type of dyslexia with a known cause. Injuries can sometimes happen when people hit their heads. Older people with **dementia** can also develop dyslexia.

KEY WORD

Dementia: a brain disease that makes it hard for people to remember things.

How Does Dyslexia Affect Your Brain?

The occipital lobe is a part of the brain that helps people understand what they see. The parietal lobe is a part of the brain that controls how people see and sense things. These lobes in the brains of people with dyslexia do not work in the same way as other people's. They are often not as busy.

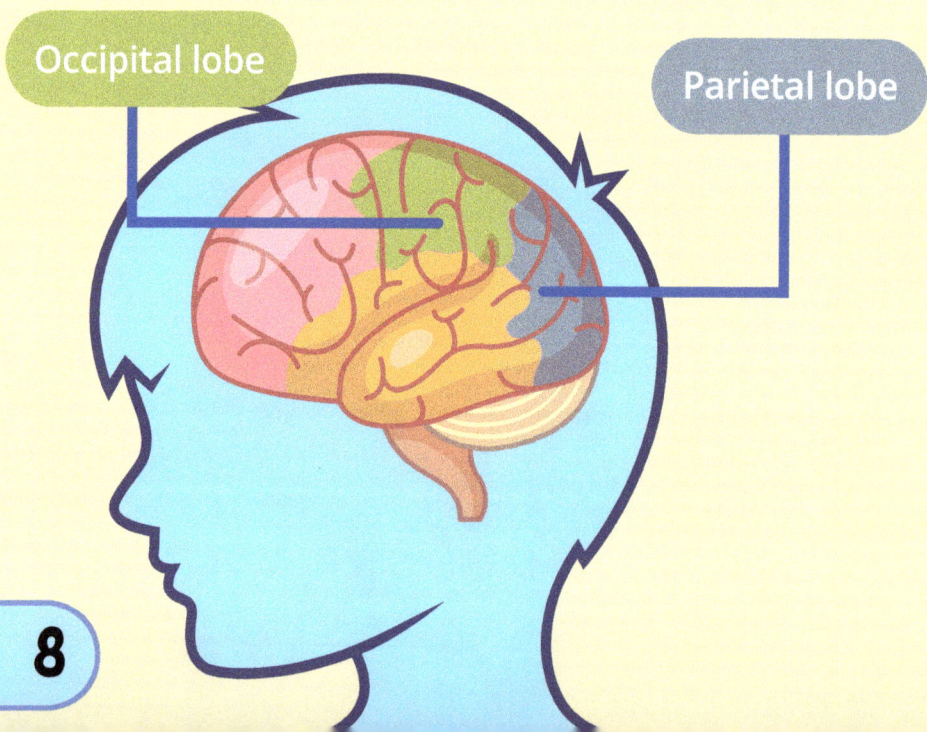

Occipital lobe

Parietal lobe

Dyslexia makes some people think in pictures instead of words. It also helps them create 3D images in their minds. This skill can be useful in science and math. Kids with dyslexia might do great in subjects that need these skills.

How Does Dyslexia Affect Your Reading?

When people with dyslexia read, they might see letters flipping or **swapping** around without warning. Words may be read differently. The word "now" could be read as "won." "Left" could be read as "felt."

KEY WORD

Swapping: changing places.

Reading out loud may feel difficult for someone with dyslexia because they might **stumble** on some words. Dyslexia can make reading a slow process. Someone might have to sound out each letter of a word or read sentences over again to fully understand them.

KEY WORD

Stumble: to trip over something while walking or speaking.

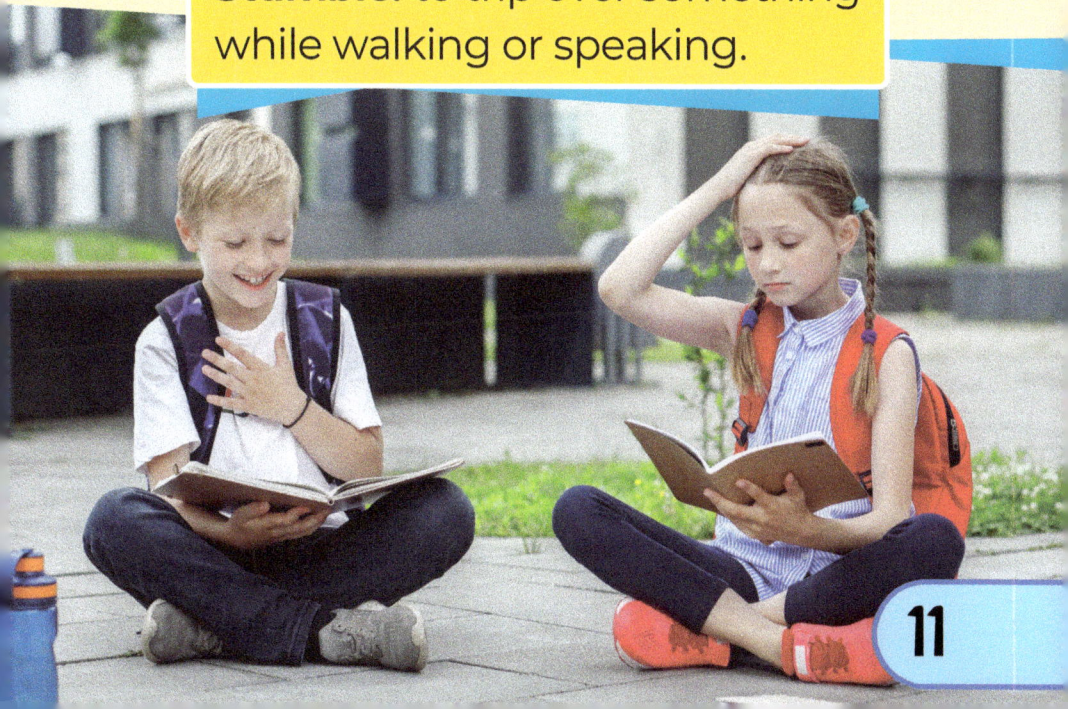

What Does Having Dyslexia Feel Like?

Dyslexia can be a hard and confusing thing to deal with. Having dyslexia can sometimes make someone feel frustrated or upset. People with dyslexia might also feel **isolated** or like other people do not understand them.

KEY WORD

Isolated: to be alone or separated from others.

Some people feel embarrassed when they cannot keep up with other people in their class. Others might feel **anxiety** about what other people think of them. People with dyslexia may feel bad about themselves or doubt their skills.

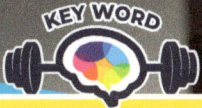

KEY WORD

Anxiety: feelings of worry and fear that are hard to control.

Does Dyslexia Go Away?

Dyslexia does not go away. But there are helpful ways to make living with dyslexia easier. Teachers can provide extra support to make reading and writing easier. Special learning tools can also be used. One simple tool is to use **fonts** that are easy for people with dyslexia to read.

KEY WORD

Fonts: different styles of letters used in writing.

With support and practice, reading and writing can become more comfortable for people with dyslexia. Some people with dyslexia find that it becomes easier as they get older. Remember, everyone learns at different speeds, and someone can get better at any time.

As children with dyslexia grow older, they may discover ways of reading and writing that work best for them.

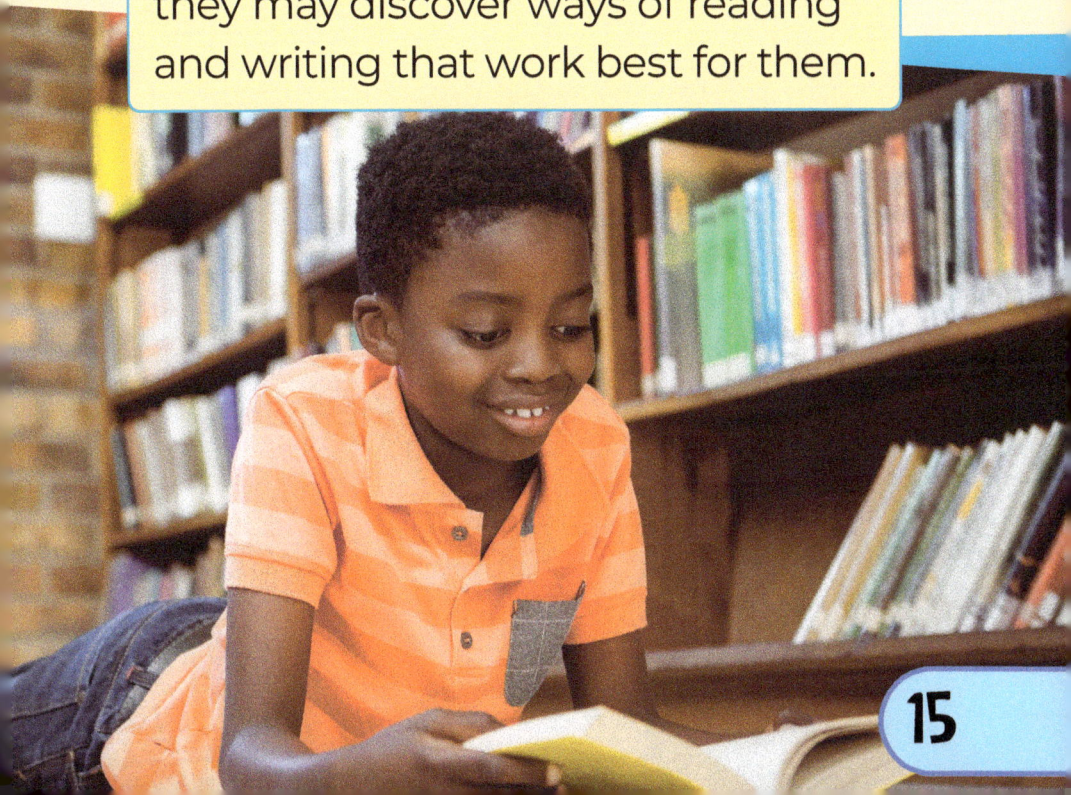

Asking for Help

If you find it difficult to read and write, ask for help as soon as possible. Talk to your teacher, parents, or a school **counselor** about what you are experiencing. They are there to support you!

KEY WORD

Counselor: a person who gives advice to others.

"I sometimes get confused when I read. Can you help me figure out why?"

"I feel frustrated when I can't spell words right. Can you give me some tips?"

"My friend has dyslexia, and I think I might have it too. How can I find out for sure?"

How to Help Others With Dyslexia

Being a good friend to someone with dyslexia means being patient and understanding. Listen to their feelings and experiences without **judgment**. Be patient and kind when they struggle with reading or writing. Offer to read together and take turns.

KEY WORD

Judgment: forming an opinion depending on what you believe.

Encourage your friend when they make progress in reading or writing. Focus on their efforts and celebrate when they reach a goal, no matter how big or small. Being a supportive friend is like being a sidekick in someone's adventure with dyslexia!

The History of Dyslexia

Rudolf Berlin was a German doctor who came up with the term "dyslexia" in 1887. He noticed reading difficulties in his patients but did not find any problems with their sight. He believed these struggles were caused by changes in the brain.

In the United States, Samuel T. Orton presented his work on word-blindness in 1925. He connected reading difficulties to the brain and linked letter understanding to sounds. He co-founded the Orton Society. It is now called the International Dyslexia Association.

The Word Blind Centre was started in 1962. It helped study dyslexia. The British Dyslexia Association and Dyslexia Institute were created in the early 1970s. These groups gave support to people with dyslexia.

Dyslexia Superheroes

Having dyslexia can sometimes make you feel like you are the only one facing challenges. But there are superheroes all over the world who have dyslexia too. These amazing heroes are helping and supporting others with dyslexia.

Magic Johnson is a great basketball player who has dyslexia. He has worked hard to beat challenges and has done great things on and off the court. He inspires others with dyslexia to believe in themselves and reach for their dreams.

Daymond John is a successful businessman from the TV show *Shark Tank*. He believes his dyslexia helped him develop his creativity and problem-solving skills. Daymond has shown others that being different can be a superpower.

Actress **Jennifer Aniston** had a hard time in school and thought she was not smart. She learned she had dyslexia as an adult. She said learning this was life changing and helped her understand why she struggled in school. She has now been in over 50 movies and TV shows and inspires many other people with dyslexia.

Dyslexia Tip 1: Reading Out Loud

Reading out loud is a good trick to help you stay focused while reading. It helps stop you from skipping words and helps you remember what you read. When you read out loud, you connect how words look to how they sound.

When you read out loud, you focus on one word at a time. It also helps you find a natural **rhythm** while reading. This makes the information in the text clearer, and you remember more of what you read.

KEY WORD

Rhythm: a pattern of sound or movement.

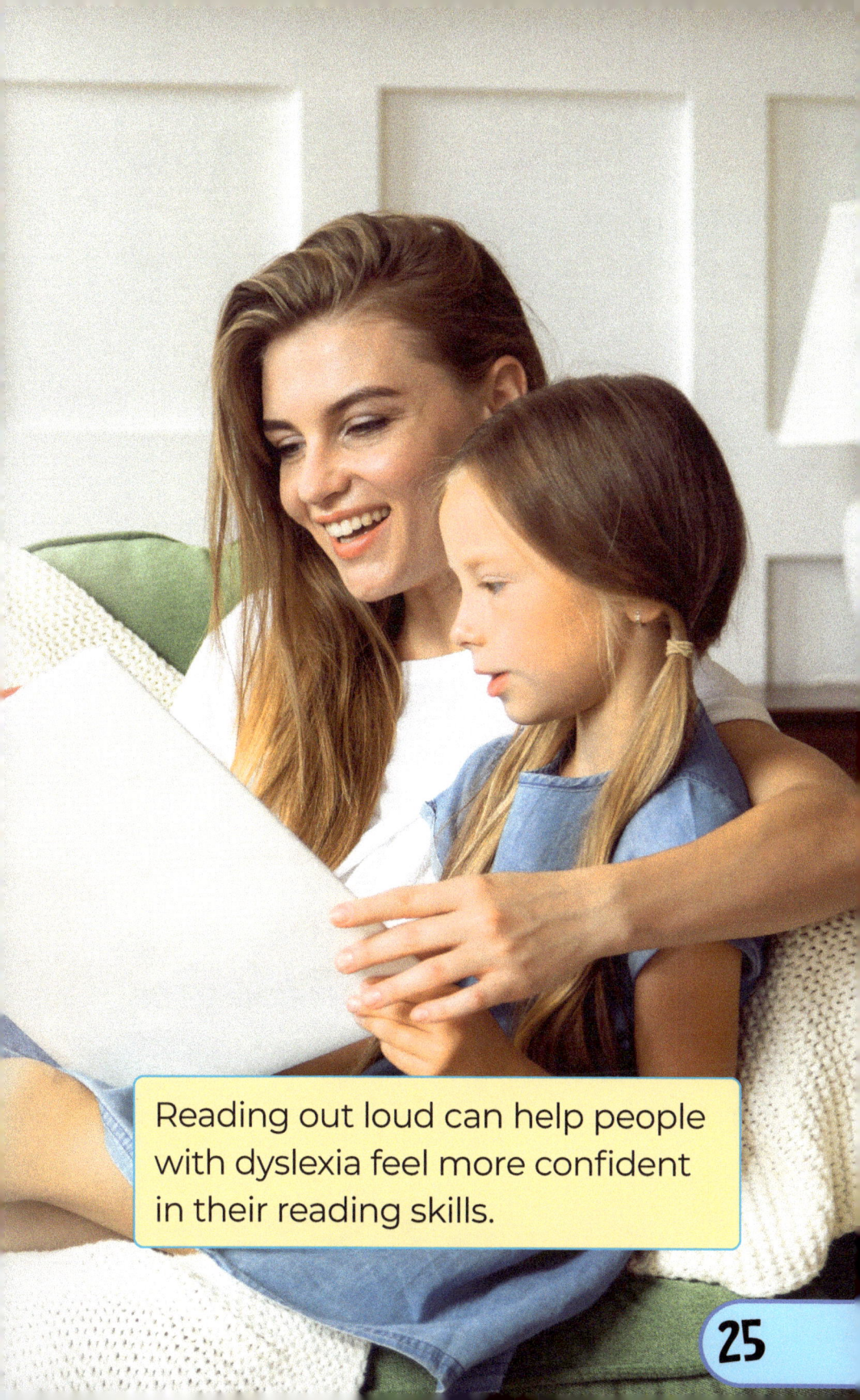

Reading out loud can help people with dyslexia feel more confident in their reading skills.

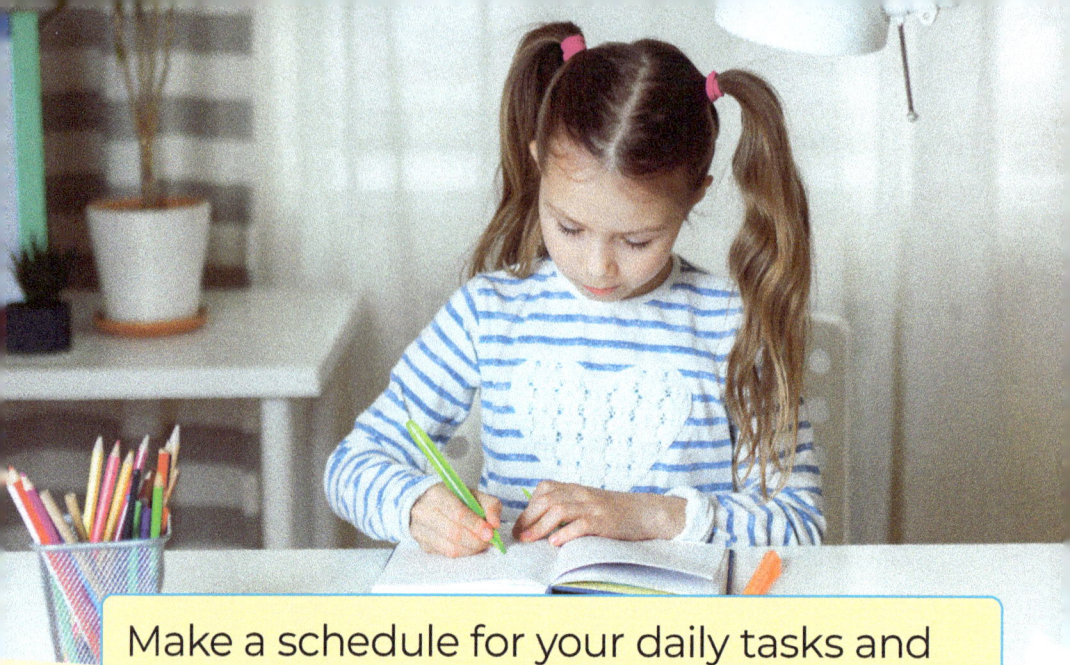

Make a schedule for your daily tasks and reward yourself when you complete them.

Dyslexia Tip 2: Using Tools and Technology

A ruler can help you read in a straight line. Markers or sticky notes can make it easier to find and remember important details when reading long texts. These tricks make reading more **physical** so it is easier to follow along.

KEY WORD

Physical: involving the body rather than the mind.

Audiobooks can help people with dyslexia focus on the meaning of the text. Text-to-speech tools can help people write words faster. Spell checkers point out words that are spelled wrong and give you ways to fix them.

KEY WORD

Audiobooks: books that are listened to instead of read.

Dyslexia Tip 3: Staying Positive

Always believe in yourself. Staying positive with dyslexia is important and can make a big difference. You are more than your dyslexia. You have unique talents and strengths. Surround yourself with supportive friends and family who understand and encourage you.

Connect with other kids or adults who have dyslexia. Share your experiences and learn from each other. With hard work and good thoughts, you can beat challenges and reach your goals!

Quiz

Test your knowledge of dyslexia by answering the following questions. The questions are based on what you have read in this book. The answers are listed on the bottom of the next page.

1 What is phonological dyslexia?

2 Which part of the brain helps people understand what they see?

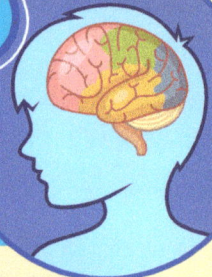

3 When people with dyslexia read, what might they see letters do without warning?

4 Can dyslexia go away completely?

5 What does Daymond John believe his dyslexia helped him do?

6 Name one helpful type of technology for people with dyslexia.

Explore Other Level 3 Readers.

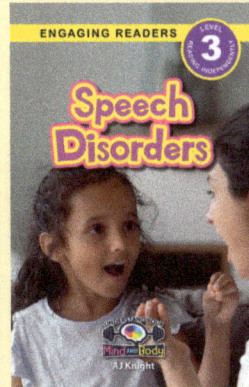

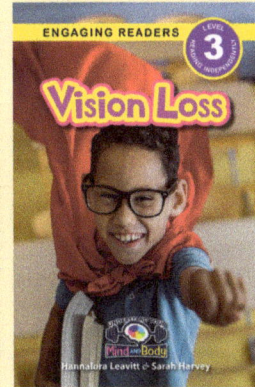

ENGAGING READERS — LEVEL 3 — **ADHD** — *AJ Knight*

ENGAGING READERS — LEVEL 3 — **Anxiety** — *Adelaide Wilder*

ENGAGING READERS — LEVEL 3 — **Asthma** — *Sarah Harvey*

ENGAGING READERS — LEVEL 3 — **Body Image** — *Adelaide Wilder*

ENGAGING READERS — LEVEL 3 — **Diabetes** — *Kit Caudron-Robinson*

ENGAGING READERS — LEVEL 3 — **Hearing Loss** — *AJ Knight*

ENGAGING READERS — LEVEL 3 — **Obesity** — *Kit Caudron-Robinson*

ENGAGING READERS — LEVEL 3 — **Speech Disorders** — *AJ Knight*

ENGAGING READERS — LEVEL 3 — **Vision Loss** — *Hannalora Leavitt & Sarah Harvey*

Visit www.engagebooks.com/readers

Answers:
1. When people struggle to decode or sound out words
2. The occipital lobe 3. Flipping or swapping around 4. No
5. Develop his creativity and problem-solving skills
6. Audiobooks, text-to-speech tools, or spell checkers.

www.ingramcontent.com/pod-product-compliance
Lightning Source LLC
Chambersburg PA
CBHW051236020426

42331CB00016B/3395